FRONT

ROCKING WITH JESUS DAILY

PORCH

GAYLE ROGERS FOSTER

MOMENTS

To Felicia,
"LORD, I am coming!"

Gayle Rogers Foster

Ps. 27:8 NLT

♡

LOVE WORTH FINDING ▪ MEMPHIS, TENNESSEE

Front Porch Moments
by Gayle Rogers Foster

Published by Love Worth Finding Ministries, Inc.
2941 Kate Bond Rd
Memphis TN 38133-4017
(800) 274-5683

Cover design by Houseal Creative

Printed in the United States of America

ENDORSEMENTS

"You have an anointing and I fully believe God is paving the way for you to speak His word to the nation as your precious father did! Praying it will come to fruition!" CARLA B.

"I need to read this reminder EVERY SINGLE DAY!" Thank you!" BRIDGET L.

"Thank you, Gayle, for always being a light in the darkness. I know that God gave me a very special gift when he put you in my life. I love you and thank you for being a messenger from Jesus to me." TRACY B.

"Your spiritual counsel and devotionals are insightful, enriching, spirit-filled, and uplifting. Glory to God!" GINGER P.

"I just love Gayle Rogers Foster. She is smart, witty, and very down to earth. I love her no-nonsense, practical, and VERY real way of relating to all of us. I look forward to hearing her every time I can. She makes me laugh out loud!" MARCIA W.

"I love real people. And, you are genuine. There is no pretense about you. I see your heart in every printed

word you pen. It's a heart bathed in the Word and Jesus. He has given you a unique personality and ability to connect with others and share in their lives. You have a holy calling. God gifted you in the womb to be His spokesperson, His agent of change." SUSAN K.

"I am thankful for you and your writing the truths of the Bible in a way that speaks to our hearts." MELISSA B.

"You always seem to know exactly what I need to hear each day." THERESA F.

"Such wisdom from God! Thank you for sharing your thoughts. They always speak to me right where I am." JOYCE M.

FOR SPEAKING ENGAGEMENTS

Contact email for inquiries about speaking:
gaylerogersfoster@gmail.com

FRONT PORCH MOMENTS

by

ELIZABETH DRAPER

In the tapestry of life, there are certain threads that weave their way into the very fabric of who we are. Gayle Foster is undeniably one of those threads in my life. From the moment my husband Randy and I met Gayle and Mike, our lives became entwined in a beautiful friendship that has lasted for more than four decades. For 31 of those years, we worked together in business, selling, training, and developing leadership.

As I reflect on our journey together, I can't help but marvel at the countless "front porch moments" we've shared—those precious instances of connection, laughter, and heartfelt conversations that have left an indelible mark on our souls.

I'm so excited about Gayle's new devotional book, "Front Porch Moments: Rocking with Jesus Daily." With a title like that, you might expect a serene, contemplative read. And while there's certainly plenty of wisdom and spiritual insight to be found within these pages, make no mistake—Gayle's infectious humor and zest for life shine through in every word. Picture this: Gayle, sitting in her rocking chair, inspiring, and challenging you with stories of everyday life infused with divine encounters. It's like having a front-row seat to the most entertaining, uplifting sermon you've ever heard—complete with a side of Southern charm and a dash of wit.

I've had the privilege of witnessing Gayle's journey firsthand, and I can attest to her uncanny ability to blend profound truths with down-to-earth humor. Whether she's sharing snippets of her own experiences or drawing inspiration from the timeless truths of Scripture, Gayle's words have a way of resonating deep within the soul. Her writing isn't just a reflection of her upbringing as the daughter of renowned pastor Adrian Rogers (and, of course, her wonderful mother, Joyce); it's a testament to her unwavering faith and her genuine desire to see lives transformed by the power of God's love.

But perhaps what I admire most about Gayle is her authenticity—the way she embraces life's ups and downs with grace and humor. She and Mike, despite being polar opposites in many ways, have weathered every storm with unwavering loyalty and commitment. And through it all, they've shown us what it means to love fiercely, laugh often, and lean on each other through thick and thin.

So, as you begin this journey through "Front Porch Moments," I encourage you to do so with an open heart and a desire to hear God's voice. Allow yourself to be transported to the front porch, where Gayle's warm hospitality and infectious laughter await. But be warned—you may just find yourself nodding in agreement, wiping away tears of laughter, and discovering profound truths, from God's Word, that speak directly to your soul.

In the end, "Front Porch Moments" isn't just a devotional book—it's an invitation to embrace the beauty of everyday moments, to seek God in the midst of the mundane, and to find joy in the journey. So, grab a glass of iced tea, pull up a chair, and get ready to start your journey of laughter, love, and life-changing encounters with Jesus. After all, as Gayle would say, there's always room for one more on the front porch.

Finding joy in the journey,

Elizabeth Draper

FRONT PORCH MOMENTS

by

GAYLE ROGERS FOSTER

Recently God sent a convictional arrow that pierced my heart. A verse from Colossians hit me between the eyes. It said, "Be sure to carry out the ministry the Lord gave you" (Colossians 4:17b). For years, I have sensed a calling to write a devotional book. God even spoke to my spirit that it would be used by Him. Through the years He has repeated that urging through many sources. Some of those sources have been you! Shamefully, I have been dodging and running from this calling.

After several decades of my business being the main course, with a sprinkling of spiritual salt and pepper, I have finally come to a place of total surrender. Jesus is now the main course instead of a condiment. I had been doing a lot of good things, but many of them were "Gayle things" and not "God things." This book is out of obedience to Him. I firmly believe that each one of us has been created with a special ministry and unique perspective in mind. In this particular volume, each devotion will end with a quote from my father, Adrian Rogers. Many lovingly refer to them as "Adrianisms." I'll give you a preview right now. My daddy said, "God has a purpose and a plan for you that no one else can fulfill." I'm finally fulfilling mine!

I know that this book may not speak equally to everyone, but I also know that there are those to whom this book will specifically and powerfully impact. If God has called me to write it, I know that God has prepared many hearts to read it. If the devotional thoughts and insights that God has given to me help you to see the things you are struggling with from a fresh perspective, then I will feel like I have fulfilled my calling. As you read the thoughts of this book, ask God to open your heart to receive the truths He has prepared specifically for you. You may be the reason He wanted me to write this.

There are also many people I want to thank. First and foremost is my husband and biggest supporter, Mike Foster. Mike, you have always believed in me and encouraged me to put my thoughts in book form. You have believed in my giftings, even when I did not. You are my complete opposite, which also makes you the interlocking piece to my puzzle. I would not be complete without your love, insight, and guidance. I don't deserve you. You are God's grace gift to me. Thank you for the countless hours of editing, proofreading, and enhancing everything I have done with your powerful insights.

I want to thank my earthly father, Adrian Rogers, for the wit and wisdom I inherited from him. My daddy has been in heaven, "kicking up gold dust on the streets of glory," since November 2005. However, he still speaks daily into multiplied thousands of lives via radio, television, and the LWF.org website. Adrian Rogers epitomized integrity, conviction, leadership, and spiritual wisdom. He preached with power.

The anointing of God was on my father's life and ministry. His dying wish for me was that I would write a book with him. God took him home before we had that chance. I have honored his wish by including an "Adrianism" or quote from him at the bottom of each devotion. This wasn't written with him, but it was written for him and includes his influence in every thought.

Daddy, you had a calling to the world, yet you always had time to build into me and love me unconditionally. I am who I am today because of you. I say with the Psalmist, "The lines are fallen unto me in pleasant places; yes, I have a goodly heritage" (Psalm 16:6, KJV).

I want to thank my precious mother, Joyce Rogers. Mother, you are a woman of character and strength. You loved Daddy so much that I thought you would fall apart when he died, but you never did. You leaned into Jesus, instead of away from Him. You never questioned your faith and never wavered in your trust. You set an example that I will spend the rest of my life trying to live up to. I am a strong woman today because of the spiritual strength I have witnessed in you.

I want to thank one of the major influencers in my life, Joan Horner. She was the co-founder of Premier Designs Jewelry, the business I was in for 31 years. She was the epitome of a lady, yet with an incredible business mind. She loved all things feminine, yet there was never a more passionate sports fanatic. She loved people and demonstrated to me that there could be no better mantra for my life than "Keeping It Personal." She loved missions, missionaries, and giving to Kingdom causes. But most of all, Joan loved God. She taught me how to let God flow through my particular giftings. Through her example, I learned there is no difference between the sacred and the secular. I was a business leader because of her mentorship. I am now a ministry leader, in large part, because of her influence. Joan showed me that both are equally sacred.

I want to thank a number of special friends, prayer warriors, mentors, and encouragers in this project. I'm going to list them in alphabetical order because there is not a way I could place any one of you above another: Mindy Abrams, Jessalyn Bailey, Nancy Bramlett, Pam Childs, Sandra Conway, Carol Ann Draper, Elizabeth Draper, Martie Dubois, Cherie Evans, Linda Forrest, Donna Gaines, Bette Stalnecker Gibson, Mitzi Gooden, Jo Gray, Rhonda Hardy, Dale Hill, Kay Horton, Colleen Ingram, Francine Ivey, Lynda Jones, Rachel Kendall, Susan Kynerd, Pat Lackey, Donna Lewis, JoAnn Manning, Ellie Marcum, Fran Miller, Debbie Nixon, Pam Pegram, Teresa Phillips, ReAnn Ring, Raenell Robinson, Vickie Saller, Gina Serrano, Pat Sexton, Gerry Sisk, Dayna Street, Melissa Terrell, Gayla Ungerer, Dode Morgan Worsham, Wendy Wotring, and Susie Wright.

Thank you to my sister, Janice Edmiston, for always believing I am better than I actually am. Thank you to the staff of Love Worth Finding. You could not be more faithful stewards of my father's ministry. And, to Bobby Lewis, please bequeath your brain to me in your will! Each person I have mentioned has played a special role in my life and in the making of this book. There are countless others of you who have encouraged me and prayed for me. There is no way I can name you all, but I deeply appreciate each one of you. I am eternally grateful for the multitude of ways you have enriched my life.

ROCKING WITH JESUS

*Listen to my cry for help, my King
and my God, for I pray to no one but
You. Listen to my voice in the morning,
Lord. Each morning I bring my
requests to You and wait expectantly.*

PSALMS 5:2-3

I can't tell you the joy I've found just sitting on my front porch these past months with Jesus. Jesus is everywhere, but I've found a secret place where His presence is so real to me that there is nowhere I would rather be than rockin' and talkin' with my Lord. If you are from the North, you can put the "g" on the ends of those words if you must, but if you do, you will forfeit your right to enjoy a glass of sweet tea while you rock.

And on my front porch, one of the blessings of my life has been to pray through the Psalms in the New Living Translation. This translation is particularly suited to the devotional language of prayer. If I were you, I wouldn't give sleep to my eyelids until I ordered a copy. Get one with the margins wide enough for you to write in. If you do, the only good thing about today's society is that it will be on your doorstep tomorrow.

I try to unplug each morning with just my rocking chair, my wide-margin NLT Bible, and a pen. I may not make it all the way through the winter, but if not, I'll find another place. Having a secret place is very important, because I know that Jesus is always there waiting on me. I know where I can find Him! I meet with Him in the mornings, but there are times when I get up from my desk and go out on my porch just to say a single sentence to Him. I can't fully explain it. You just have to experience it. His presence is everywhere, but there are places where it is so thick you can cut it with a knife.

You don't have to do this the exact way I do it, but if you don't have a method of your own, I encourage you to try mine. I take each chapter in the Psalms, sentence by sentence, and turn it into a first-person dialogue with God. Just change the word "He" to "You" as you talk directly to Him. I do it out loud. I know He can hear my thoughts, but it just seems more real when I speak it out loud. And even more importantly, when I speak out loud, I don't rush. When I go to my secret place and pray the Psalms or other chapters of the Bible back to God, there is no place I'd rather be. I'm not just trying to check it off my to-do list of daily spiritual disciplines.

As I write this, I am praying through Psalm 19. The very first verse says, "The heavens proclaim the glory of God. The skies display His craftsmanship." I pray that back to God by saying, "The heavens proclaim Your glory, O God. The skies proclaim Your craftsmanship." Today, when I did that, I camped out there for a bit. The words of David give you a starting place, not necessarily an ending place.

Psalm 19:2 says, "Day after day they continue to speak; night after night they make Him known." As I prayed verse two back to God, the truth of that verse also prompted a prayer of intercession for a loved one. The Psalms are prayers in and of themselves, but they are also prayer prompts. And so, I prayed that night after night the moon and the stars would make God known to that particular person that I love.

In the past, I always found it difficult to know what to pray and even more difficult to maintain my focus. Praying through the Book of Psalms, instead of only reading it, has been a key that has unlocked an ancient door to a secret garden. And what beautiful and fragrant flowers are inside that garden.

I could go on and on and on about the joys and delights of this treasured time with Him. Most of the devotions I have written in this little book were written immediately after my time alone with Jesus on my front porch. I just picked up my phone while still sitting in my rocking chair and very simply pecked out what I felt like God had just said to me.

But hearing from God isn't something reserved only for me. Yes, I love my secret place. You may not even have a front porch, but there is a secret place for you as well. God's invitations are for anyone who will respond. There is no more important request than the one found in Psalm 27:8: "My heart has heard You say, 'Come and talk with Me.' And my heart responds, 'LORD, I am coming.'"

He has invited you to rock with Him and talk with Him. He is waiting for your response.

....

Getting into the Bible prompts us to pray.

ADRIAN ROGERS

GOD KNOWS WHAT
YOU NEED

*Three different times I begged the Lord
to take it away. Each time He said,
"My grace is all you need. My
power works best in weakness."*

2 CORINTHIANS 12:8-9A

A couple of years ago God ended a business I dearly loved. At the time, I didn't see it as being the hand of God, but it was. It ended abruptly. In and of itself, there wasn't anything wrong with my business. In fact, there were a lot of beautiful things about it. When it ended, I wasn't prepared. At the time it happened, I'm not certain I could have let it go on my own, even if God had told me to do so. That ought to have been a sign, right there.

I didn't realize it, but very slowly and silently I had begun to worship the gift God had given to me, instead of the giver of the gift. Satan cunningly knows how to turn beautiful things into idols. So, God gave me another gift. He gave me the gift of a new beginning. It was a gift I didn't want. But,

5

surprise, God knew best! Even though I didn't want it, it was the perfect gift for me.

I am so grateful for the emptiness that caused me to seek His fullness. There is nothing like a desperately empty hole in the pit of your stomach. Desperation causes you to seek answers like nothing else. And there were no answers. It seemed as if He walled me in on four sides and then pulled the bottom out. I found that there was nowhere to look, but up. But praise God, when I did look up, I discovered that the Giver of the gift was infinitely better than the gift He had given to me. I learned to worship Him and hold everything else, even the good things, loosely—people, possessions, positions. All of them need to be held loosely. Tightness of grip squeezes the goodness out of even the best things and turns lemonade right back into lemons.

I am so grateful for the loneliness that caused me to crave His presence. My friends, my network, my tribe, and seemingly, my purpose were all tied up in my business. I went from having the consistent adrenaline rush of people to the stifling loneliness of silence. But in that silence, I found a Friend who had been waiting for my attention. And oh, what a Friend He has been. I had drowned Him out by the noise and replaced Him with hundreds of shallow substitutes. And I came to discover in my own experience the reality of something I had heard someone say years ago. "What God will bless as a supplement, He'll curse as a substitute." When I had nowhere to go, I found that there was nowhere I needed to go. He was inside of me. He was in front of me and behind me. He was surrounding me. He was looking down on me. He was underneath me supporting me. He was all I needed and more. Jesus is now my very closest friend, and there is nothing sweeter than the solitude of having Him all to myself.

I am so grateful for the poverty that forced me to discover true riches. I had what the world calls success. And success doesn't require a lot of faith. There was money in the bank and what I thought was security for my future. I didn't feel the need to trust God for my day-to-day needs. Money was deposited like clockwork into my account on the 10th of every month. Then abruptly, it stopped. It never crossed my mind that was even possible. I assumed it would go on forever. I had replaced faith with residual income. And not only that, I had also forgotten what true riches really were. Now, every dollar that has been taken away has been replaced tenfold with joy and peace. My spiritual bank account is overflowing, and I can't stop singing, "I'd rather have Jesus than silver or gold. I'd rather have Him than have riches untold."

I am so grateful that He took away who I was and showed me who He could be in me. This brings tears to my eyes. I thought I had it together. I was good at being me. I studied leadership and took "Strength-Finders" tests. I operated in my "lane" and used my skill set. But God wasn't impressed. I found myself playing "Spades" with Him. Every time I laid down an Ace of Hearts, or Diamonds, or Clubs, He trumped me with a 2 or 3 or 4 of Spades. I went from "being all that and a bag of chips" to a carton of expired milk. I found out that God wasn't interested in my strengths at all.

He wanted my weakness. He wanted my emptiness. He wanted me to let go of who I was and what others thought of me. I was so filled with me that all I was accomplishing was what any other strong-willed, self-driven person could accomplish—things that will become wood, hay, and stubble at the judgment.

God had to break me down to empty me, clean me up, and fill me with His presence and His power. My pastor's wife, Donna Gaines, told me that if you aren't broken, there are no openings for God's light to shine through. Oh, there are still a few personality quirks and inclinations that remain, but for the most part, I don't even recognize myself. And that's a very good thing. In the words of the old gospel song, "I lost it all to find everything." He knew what I needed. I didn't want it then. I wouldn't trade it now.

You can trust Him, too. I believe it was Toby Mac who originally said, "We ask God to change our situation, not knowing He put us in the situation to change us." Just trust Him.

. . . .

I don't find the will of God. The will of God finds me, and I respond to it.

ADRIAN ROGERS

FILLING UP AND POURING OUT

*The Holy Spirit said to Philip, "Go over
and walk along beside the carriage."
Philip ran over and heard the man reading
from the prophet Isaiah. Philip asked, "Do
you understand what you are reading?"*

ACTS 8:29-30

A wise person said, "If you stay ready, you don't have
to get ready." That's good advice because most opportunities have a short shelf life. In business, you
will miss your window to act if your due diligence
isn't done before you see the opportunity. In much
the same way, if you don't immediately respond to
the still, soft voice of the Holy Spirit telling you to
speak a word into someone, they will have moved on.
You intersect with numerous people in the day-to-day
activities of your life. If there is no alertness in your
spirit to Divine opportunities, those opportunities
will quickly vanish like circles on a pond when a
stone is thrown. The sad fact is that most people
are so absorbed in the affairs of everyday life that

9

they are oblivious to the Divine appointments that were missed.

On the other hand, if you know there is nothing wasted in God's economy, you will be hyper-alert to Divine opportunities that accompany each person who crosses your path. If you have prepared spiritually, you should be actively looking for people who need what God has just put into you.

People don't take advantage of opportunities because they get lucky. They take advantage of opportunities because they are ready and watching for them. Assignments from God rarely have a lead time. Generally, "God-moments" are found in fleeting fragments of time we have with the person who "happens" to be standing next to us for a few minutes or sitting beside us for a few hours.

When you continuously abide in Christ, the Holy Spirit will supernaturally position people into the exact place and time to be able to receive a word that He has given to you to pass on to them. It won't be luck. It won't be happenstance. It will be a Divine Appointment. And preparation for these Divine Appointments is a lifestyle, not a seminary class. When one person is seeking God, at the same time, God's eyes are searching the earth to find the nearest believer who has already prepared in private and is willing to be poured out in public.

Yes, go on mission trips, but 99% of the people you are called to speak into are seated in the cubicle next to you, or across the table from you. Your responsibility is to consistently allow God to pour Himself into you each day. You should have a constant awareness that whatever He has poured into you will, in turn, be needed by someone else who will become your Divine assignment in the very near future. God's responsibility is to find the match. He will place those people into your path who need what He has purposely just poured into you. When that happens, it is never a coincidence. God is the master of pairing your preparation with His Divine orchestration.

Your life should be a continual loop of filling up and pouring back out. It should be as consistent as the tide coming in and going out, or the sun rising and setting. You will always see what you are intentionally looking for. Live your life with the assumption that God is preselecting specific people to cross your pathway each day. When you are on the lookout for His assignments, as a servant and a steward, you will be overwhelmed by the way God will use you for His glory. Be spiritually prepared and instantly responsive.

....

"If you wonder why some folks are used and you're not used, just get yourself usable, and God will wear you out. Oh, the eyes of the Lord are searching to and fro in the earth trying to find men, women, boys, and girls that He can use."

ADRIAN ROGERS

SATAN IS LYING IN THE AREA OF YOUR GIFTINGS

In His grace, God has given us different
gifts for doing certain things well.

ROMANS 12:6A

I have always thought that Holley Armstrong Gerth is a thought-provoking author. She wrote: "The enemy is lying to us in the area of our giftings. I think the purpose of the lies is to hold us back from who we're created to be and what we're called to do."

I am convinced that what Holley has said is truth! I know personally that there are many times Satan tells me that I'm not good in areas where God has actually supernaturally gifted me. I've seen him do the same thing to others, as well. Even at this moment, He may be causing you to doubt what are actually your strongest giftings.

If Satan can get you to doubt your strengths and your effectiveness in the areas of your calling, then he has effectively neutralized your influence for the kingdom. Why are we so easily duped and self-absorbed by this obsession with our own inadequacy? We are created in the image of Almighty God!

I encourage you to stand up and be mighty in the areas of your giftings. But do it in the power of the Holy Spirit. Romans 12:6-8 says: "In His grace, God has given us different gifts for doing certain things well. So, if God has given you the ability to prophesy, speak out with as much faith as God has given you. If your gift is serving others, serve them well. If you are a teacher, teach well. If your gift is to encourage others, be encouraging. If it is giving, give generously. If God has given you leadership ability, take the responsibility seriously. And if you have a gift for showing kindness to others, do it gladly." That, my friend, is the Holy Scripture, and it's pretty plain!

To poor mouth who you are is to disrespect the Giver of your gift. You are gifted, not because you are superior. Everyone is gifted. It isn't just you. You are gifted because of God's grace, not because you are more special. And you are only gifted to do certain things well. You are not gifted to do everything well. When you try to do everything, you actually keep the person who is gifted in that area from being able to utilize the gifting God has given her. Equally so, when you don't do what you are gifted at doing, you leave a gaping hole. It's so simple. Just do what God has gifted you to do! And remember, according to the Scripture, showing kindness is just as important as leadership ability.

I will also say that if you see someone who you believe is more gifted in a certain area than you, it doesn't excuse you. Fine steakhouses and fast food joints can both serve up some tasty food. There are many ladies who are no doubt exponentially more gifted than me in the area of teaching. My pastor's wife is probably a more gifted teacher than 99.9% of the people on the face of the earth. But that does not excuse me from using the gift of teaching God has given to me. It didn't excuse the servants in Matthew 25:14-28 who were only given one and two talents when the other servant was given five. Each one of the servants was expected to use and multiply the talent that he was given. The reward was the exact same for the servant who multiplied the two talents he was given as it was for the servant who multiplied the five talents he was given. God looks at obedience, not equal ability. And God doesn't cut any slack for the one who was only given one talent. In the parable, the one who buried the one single talent he had been given because of fear, wasn't given a pass. He was given a very harsh punishment. This is a serious matter.

God has gifted every single one of you. And along with that gifting, He has also equipped and empowered you. To deny that is not humility, it is unbelief. Satan is the one who wants you to doubt it. And as Neil Anderson so eloquently says, "Satan has no power over you except the power of the lie."

Take courage and do not fear. Take the next step that God is prompting you to take. He has already placed what you will need inside of you. It may be dormant now, but it will be activated by the indwelling power of the Holy Spirit. "For I can do everything through Christ, who gives me strength" (Philippians 4:13). "He will not fail you or forsake you" (1 Chronicles 28:20b).

To not use your gifting is to be a poor steward. It is false humility. It is failing to do the part you were created to do in the kingdom of God. Never forget what the Apostle Paul said in Ephesians 2:10: "For we are God's masterpiece. He has created us anew in Christ Jesus, so we can do the good things He planned for us long ago."

"Humility is knowing what I am, acknowledging that God made me that way and giving Him glory for it."

ADRIAN ROGERS

WAITING FOR A
SPECIAL TREAT

Listen to my voice in the morning,
LORD. Each morning I bring my
request to you and wait expectantly.

PSALM 5:3

I know that most of you have had a beloved dog. Probably all the dogs you've had have been beloved. You love your dog because your dog uncondition- ally loves you. Let me tell you about my dog. He was a Dalmatian named Tucker. He was so special you would have been able to "spot" him in a crowd. Sorry, bad joke. Tucker, like many Dalmatians, was deaf in one ear. But that other ear was something to behold.

Tucker would be in the basement, minding his own dog business (hopefully not doing his business). And if I was upstairs in the kitchen opening a cereal box, even though he only had one good ear, that dog could hear even the faintest crinkling sound coming from that box. I mean, he could hear even a fainter sound than a "Horton Hears a Who" sound. And, like lightning, Tucker would bound up the stairs and stare me down with drool coming down his mouth until I gave him a treat. Even though he was half-deaf, I believe he could have heard the sound of the cereal box opening from down the street and around the corner.

I think that is exactly what it means when we are told to wait on God. I will tell you with certainty that Tucker wouldn't have ever gotten anything from me if he had not bounded upstairs and stared at me in anticipation. He just wouldn't have. I would have eaten all that cereal by myself. Now don't call the animal rights people. I would have fed him his meal when the time came and filled his bowl with water, but he would have missed the treat. However, when he was just waiting, staring, and anticipating, there was no way that I ever would not have given him some extra goodness. It's not humanly possible. And it's also not heavenly possible.

Put this down big. You will absolutely miss out on the treats that God will give to you if you are not waiting in His presence. But when you are there in the early morning hours or in the night watch, waiting with your eyes of your heart fixed on Him in anticipation, He will always love and lavish in return.

Are there days you never received what you could have had because you were too caught up playing with your little squeaky toy?

....

"You deny yourself when you don't pray. Prayer is the key that unlocks heaven's treasury."

ADRIAN ROGERS

18

HE IS COMING
FOR YOU

If a man has a hundred sheep and one
of them gets lost, what will he do?
Won't he leave the ninety-nine others
in the wilderness and go to search for
the one that is lost until he finds it?

LUKE 15:4

From our human perspective, it is easy to think that God is probably occupied with something far more important than us. After all, "He's got the whole world in His hands!" But one of the most unfathomable truths is that it absolutely doesn't matter that God is running the entire universe. He still cares about every tiny detail in your life. If that statement was in the Psalms it would say, "Selah" after it. In case you ever wondered, in the Psalms, Selah means, "Stop, and think about that!" Though some people still swear that it was what David said when he broke a harp string.

Psalms 139:1-4 says: "O LORD, You have examined my heart and know everything about me. You know when I sit down or stand up. You know my thoughts even when I'm far away. You see me when I travel and when I rest at home. You know everything I do. You know what I am going to say even before I say it, LORD."

Psalms 139:17-18, says: "How precious are Your thoughts about me, O God. They cannot be numbered. I can't even count them; they outnumber the grains of sand! And when I wake up, You are still with me." Just let it sink in that God knows everything about you and it doesn't disgust Him. It doesn't repel Him. His thoughts about you are not thoughts of judgment and condemnation. They are thoughts of mercy and restoration. He can't stop thinking about how much He loves you.

He knows when you are lost and lonely. He knows when you are hurting and helpless. In Luke 15:3-7 Jesus tells the story of a shepherd who has 100 sheep, and one of them gets lost. He doesn't ignore that one sheep for the sake of the greater good. No, He leaves the others to search for the one who is lost. Someone has said, "Jesus leaving 99 to find one seems crazy until you are that one." And if you are lost, He has gone to find you. You can count on it.

The amazing thing is that the things you think will cause the Shepherd to leave you behind are actually the very things that ignite His heart to go and find you. You need saving and He is the Savior. You need healing and He is the healer. You need to be redeemed and He is the Redeemer. Your need is His rallying cry. What you think would make Him turn away is what makes Him run toward you. The entire reason He left the glories of heaven and came to earth was "to seek and save those who are lost" (Luke 19:10).

This is such a strange paradox. Your wandering does not disqualify you from His purpose for you. In reality, your wandering allows Him to fulfill His purpose for you. It was the reason He came.

He would have come if you had been the only one. He will still come, even if your shame is so deep that you are convinced you have forfeited all hope of ever deserving His grace. Listen, ALL grace is undeserved. That's the meaning of the word. Feeling that you don't qualify only means that you do qualify. He will find you no matter how far away you have wandered. He never took His eyes off you.

He won't come because of who you are. He will come because of who He is. He is the Shepherd, the Seeker, the Savior.

....

"I want to tell you, God loves you! The Good Shepherd is seeking you. The Holy Spirit is shining light on you. And God the Father has His arms open wide."

ADRIAN ROGERS

CHALLENGE YOUR THOUGHTS, CHANGE YOUR LIFE

They traded the truth about God for a lie.

ROMANS 1:25A

Each day your brain is bombarded with thoughts–some true, some lies. When these inevitable thoughts come, they automatically follow the beaten path of ruts that have formed in your brain through repetition and acceptance. They follow that path regardless of whether it leads to life or to death.

If your thoughts are based on truth, then every new, correct thought will build a pathway in your mind that becomes so aligned with truth that your default thinking literally becomes the Mind of Christ. On the contrary, if your thoughts are based on lies, you are in grave danger. You will end up forever lost in a jungle of despair and defeat if you do not take the machete of the Word of God and begin to forge new trails through your mental wilderness. His word is "sharper than the sharpest two-edged sword" (Hebrews 4:12b). You must recognize, reject, and replace the lies of the enemy with the truth of God's Word.

Most people never challenge their own thoughts. They don't think about what they think. It is extremely dangerous to listen to yourself, but it is very prudent to speak yourself! There is a difference. Most people are naive simpletons who are easily duped. Every thought you have does not come from God. Satan has targeted your mind with intentional lies. And you even come up with some doozies all by yourself. Each thought, whether it be from Satan himself or just your unsanctified mind, must be carefully compared with God's Word. A mentally lazy person is easy picking for your shrewd enemy.

You cannot help a wrong thought that runs through your mind any more than you can be accountable for receiving a spam email. Wrong thoughts and computer spam both attempt to accomplish the same thing. Computer spam attempts to trick you into opening it, reading it, and following the links down the rabbit hole of scam or pornography. Most of the time, spam is easily recognized by the title or the sender. Sometimes just reading the heading is enough to get "mud" splashed on you. You didn't invite it. You didn't sin when you received it. But you still need to delete it and clean up your computer. Block it, if possible. You don't need to confess to getting filthy spam emails as a sin. But if you read them and open the accompanying links, you do. It becomes a sin when you look at the contents out of curiosity.

Like spam, when wrong thoughts come, just delete them. Then immediately and thoroughly wash your mind out with the truth of God's Word.

....

"A clock that is five minutes off is far more dangerous than a clock that is five hours off."

ADRIAN ROGERS

HOW EMPATHETIC ARE YOU?

He will not fight or shout or raise His voice in public. He will not crush the weakest reed or put out a flickering candle.

MATTHEW 12:19-20A

When you hear that someone is sick or suffering because of a wrong choice or a self-inflicted wound, do you hurt *with* them? Or, do you get all "judgy" and lecture them as to why it is happening? That's what Job's "friends" did. If you want to lecture and instruct, you are going to miss the most important opportunity you will ever have to minister.

Nothing will make a person withdraw faster than a lecture in their time of need. It simply won't be received. This has absolutely nothing to do with whether or not you are right, or whether or not what you share would have helped. The event has already happened. Is your goal to make them feel worse? Are you trying to swat flies off their head with a hammer? A lecturer passes out judgment and blame at someone's lowest point.

Hurting people need empathy, grace, compassion, kindness, and tenderness. What they need from you are eyes that are filled with tears and arms that are ready to embrace. They don't need a lesson on cause and effect. Matthew 12:19-20a describes Jesus this way: "He will not fight or shout or raise His voice in public. He will not crush the weakest reed or put out a flickering candle."

Yes, there is a time for strong prophetic judgment, but that time is not when a heart has been plowed by adversity and in desperate need to be planted with seeds of grace. In Psalm 25:18 David pleads with God. He cries out, "Feel my pain and see my trouble. Forgive all my sins." He says, God, instead of judgment, please give me empathy and forgiveness.

When a hurting person is helped through a hard situation by a kind and compassionate friend, they will be open to wise guidance after they are safely on the other side. You don't tell a person who is drowning that they should have enlisted in a swimming class when they were young. If someone is already hurting, the last thing you need to do is wound their spirit. At that critical time, their spirit is fragile like the flickering candle that was talked about earlier. It takes great care not to extinguish it. If you are not gentle, their spirit will close up to you faster than you can imagine. And if it does, it will take a long time for there to be enough trust to get it to open up again.

Your goal should be to do whatever is possible to keep their spirit open so that you can pour in the healing balm of the love of Christ. No one cares if you are right. They only care if you are loving. To have any opportunity at all to minister, keep your opinions on what they did to cause their own misery to yourself. Obviously, they caused their own problems. We all have. If you have found grace, your sole desire in life should be to pass it on. Never forget that "People don't care how much you know until they know how much you care."

....

"Mercy is sympathy with legs."

ADRIAN ROGERS

WHY ARE YOU
STILL HERE?

But if I live, I can do more
fruitful work for Christ.

PHILIPPIANS 1:22A

There is not a single reason for God to have given you breath again today unless there is something specific left for you to do. If you woke up this morning, there's a reason. The Apostle Paul knew this. He said in Philippians 1:21-25: "For to me, living means living for Christ, and dying is even better. But if I live, I can do more fruitful work for Christ. So I really don't know which is better. I'm torn between two desires: I long to go and be with Christ, which would be far better for me. But for your sakes, it is better that I continue to live. Knowing this, I am convinced that I will remain alive so I can continue to help all of you grow and experience the joy of your faith."

If you aren't doing what Paul said, there is no reason for you to be here.

Of course, you have purpose. Of course, you have a calling. Of course, you have Divine appointments and assignments for today. You dare not be careless or oblivious to the needs around you. You cannot be callous to the hurts of others. If God has chosen to leave you here another day as His ambassador, it is only because you have an assignment to fulfill. You have a Master to please. There is at least one person who needs to hear what you have to say or receive what you have to give. That person will be within your reach today.

You may not even know who it is before your day begins or who it was after it ends. It may be someone you don't even have a clue is watching you from a distance. And even if you are unable to speak directly to anyone today, you can make a difference through your intercession. You may be left here on earth to intercede for somebody. You know for certain that there are people who are assigned to you by God because you are still here.

Therefore, whatever you do, make certain you fill up with Jesus every morning. You need a fresh word from Him each day to speak into others. Determine to be sensitive, alert, and available to the people God brings into your path. Commit to be faithful to your Lord and Master.

If you are moping around thinking you have nothing left in the tank and nothing of any value to offer to anyone, you are so very wrong. That is the same as telling God that He doesn't know what He is doing. When He is finished with you, He will take you. If you are 105 years old and still here, I would venture to say that your hospice nurse needs to find Jesus.

....

"Don't give God instructions;
just report for duty!"

ADRIAN ROGERS

HE HAS A SURPRISE TRIP PLANNED FOR YOU

The LORD had said to Abram, "Leave
your native country, your relatives,
and your father's family, and go to
the land that I will show you. I will
make you into a great nation. I will
bless you and make you famous, and
you will be a blessing to others."

GENESIS 12:1-2

Did you know that God knows more about you than you even know about yourself? He knows things that you will be crazy about that, to date, you've never even heard of. He knows songs you will love that haven't yet been written. He knows foods you've never had the nerve to try, that you are going to absolutely love when you finally take a bite. There are things He knows you are capable of doing that you wouldn't believe, even if He told you with an audible voice.

This God, who knows you so well, has planned a trip for you with a secret itinerary. Only someone with such intimate knowledge could possibly design this dream trip. There is no doubt you will love it.

In fact, you will love it more than if you had been given an unlimited budget and told you could plan it yourself. Your eyes have never seen and your ears have never heard all that God has in store for you.

Certainly, there will be challenging activities. You don't want to be bored to death. But the activities He has planned will be situations that will utilize your giftings. When you employ your faith, His power will activate your giftings. You will overcome and even excel. The things you will need have already been put inside of you. The challenges you will face are lopsidedly stacked in your favor. This trip is designed exclusively for you with your strengths and your tastes in mind. It isn't a cookie-cutter group tour.

Of course, God isn't going to tell you the details in advance. That would ruin the surprise. He doesn't need to tell you. It is a great adventure. He already knows you will love it. He made you. He knows every thought in your head before you even think it. He knows the sights you will love before you even see them. He knows the people you will emotionally bond with before you even meet them. He knows the situations that will allow you to excel. He can't wait to put you into those situations where you will win. Why can't you relax and trust?

Be like Abraham. Just accept His invitation. Pack your bag. Put on the blindfold and get in the car. If you are living out your days with no purpose, then reach out your hand and accept the golden ticket He is offering. Do you really want tomorrow to be identical to yesterday? There is an exhilarating life of purpose and meaning waiting for you. There is only one caveat. You have to be willing to step into the unknown.

....

> **"God only wants for us what we would want for ourselves if we were smart enough to want it."**
>
> ADRIAN ROGERS

FRONT PORCH MOMENTS

38

OPEN HANDS

Take your son, your only son—yes,
Isaac, whom you love so much—and go
to the land of Moriah. Go and sacrifice
him as a burnt offering on one of the
mountains, which I will show you.

GENESIS 22:2

I think about the advice given for true love: "If you really love someone, let him go. If he doesn't return, he was never really yours to begin with." I like what a cynical person said even better: "If he does return, let him go again. No one else wanted him either." But seriously, I can't tell you how hard it is for a person who likes to be in control to loosen their grip. After all, isn't the opposite of being in control, being out of control? You would think so, but no. Actually, the opposite of you being in control is for God to be in control. So instead of asking yourself, "Would you like to be in control or out of control?" the better question is, "Who would be better at handling this, you or God?"

My spiritual growth took an exponential leap forward when I began to open both of my palms to

God every morning. Literally. Everything began to change when I said, "Take anything You want out of my hands. Take anything I love more than I love You. Take anything that will harm me. Take anything that will stand in the way of being all I can be for You." That is still a terrifying thing to do.

On my best days, I think, "But please don't take my grandchildren." On my most spiritually shallow days, I think, "Please don't take the Atlanta Braves." The wonderful revelation I have found is that God isn't waiting to inflict pain on me. To be sure, there are things He has taken out of my hands. But more than anything, He is eager to swap out something in my hands for something far better. Psalm 145:16 says, "You open Your hand. You satisfy the hunger and thirst of every living thing." That says to me, when I open my hand to Him, that's when He opens His hand to me. That's the reason I always keep my hands open when I do this. I say, "I want anything You put back in them. This time, I will be a steward of what You give to me."

I think about the boy with the five small barley loaves and two small fish in John 6. He was the only one who thought to make lunch preparations ahead of time. Why should he give his lunch to all the lazy people who didn't prepare? In Mark Batterson's book, "The Grave Robber," he says the fact that a young child would share anything may have been a bigger miracle than Jesus multiplying the fish and bread. But when he opened his hand and gave it to Jesus, it was multiplied and fed about twenty thousand people, including the women and children. And just to show off, Jesus made sure there were twelve baskets left over to send home with each of the disciples as a reminder.

When you pry your fingers off the things you are grasping, He may take them away. I can't guarantee that He won't. He will definitely take out things that are wrong and sinful. In addition, He will probably take out the things that could have been good if they had been kept in the proper priority. Many times, when He takes out good things, He is doing so in order to rearrange them. He may give them back if He can trust you to keep them in the right order. There are some broken things He takes out and repairs before He returns them. I have found that the safest way for God to allow me to keep the things I love is for me to hold them loosely and never love them more than I love Jesus.

What I know for sure is that I have never held more beautiful treasures in my hands than when I let Him do the choosing for me. I recently saw a picture on the internet illustrating why toddlers should not be allowed to make their own choices. On one side of the table was an Oreo cookie, and on the other side was a stack of hundred-dollar bills. The toddler chooses the Oreo every time. A parent should make that choice and not a child. When you open your hands every day to God, you are letting the only One who knows what something is truly worth choose for you. The only things He will ever take from you are things that are not for your good, your growth, or His glory. When He asked Abraham to sacrifice Isaac, He wasn't really going to take him. It was only a test. What He will always take are counterfeits. He always wants to replace counterfeits with true riches. Basically, it boils down to this. If you will trust Him, He will trust you. Luke 16:11 says: "And if you are untrustworthy about worldly wealth, who will trust you with the true riches of heaven?"

....

"God is not some cosmic killjoy. Every time He says, 'Thou shalt not,' He's simply saying, 'Don't hurt yourself.' And every time He says, 'Thou shalt,' He's saying, 'Help yourself to happiness.'"

ADRIAN ROGERS

DONATING MASTERPIECES

For we are God's masterpiece.
He has created us anew in Christ Jesus,
so we can do the good things He
planned for us long ago.

EPHESIANS 2:10

Years ago, I had the privilege of visiting a magnificently beautiful home. It was furnished with artwork and sculptures that obviously belonged in a museum. To say I was in awe is an understatement.

During my visit, I found out that these were indeed incredibly valuable works of art. They had been pre-appraised and pre-approved for inclusion in exclusive museums. The extremely knowledgeable and savvy homeowners purchased these prized pieces at auction for a considerable sum of money, but they were still purchased at only a fraction of their actual appraised value. My very small and sheltered mind was absolutely blown when I was told that, in reality, these valuable pieces didn't cost the homeowners a dime. Rather, the homeowners would literally make money by purchasing them and turning around and donating them after they had enjoyed them for a time. This is because the legally allowable tax deduction they would receive was more valuable than the actual cost of strategically purchasing them at the right price.

Don't go out and try that as a non-professional. The museums only accepted masterpieces. The price of each piece and the acceptance of the artwork were pre-determined before the actual purchase ever took place. It wasn't a gamble. It was a very carefully crafted and certain profit.

My friends constantly rotated a stream of museum-quality paintings, sculptures, and antiquities on the walls and in the hallways of their residence. They enjoyed them for a few months or a few years and then replaced them with other masterpieces when they passed them on to their final destination. They profited from, and also personally enjoyed, everything they gave away.

That is how it works with us. Yes, we are God's masterpiece. But He also gives us masterpieces in the form of insights, blessings, words of encouragement, and testimonies. We do get to enjoy what He gives to us. We get to hang these masterpieces on our walls and look at them for a bit. But we are always to be looking for the perfect person who needs what He has given to us. All we are is a holding area. We are a beautiful warehouse that gets to enjoy glorious gifts for a tiny bit of time before they are given to others. That isn't sad, because each day brings new treasures. His blessings are always changing, and the scenery never gets old.

What masterpiece has God given to you today? He will allow you to benefit from His insights and His blessings. But then He will prompt you to pass them on to someone else. His supply is limitless and there will always be something new to take their place. And when you are a steward and not an owner, those priceless treasures of heaven are available to you without cost.

....

"I tell people to keep the faith. And that's true. But we should also give it away. If you have no desire to give it away, perhaps you ought to give it up."

ADRIAN ROGERS

FRONT PORCH MOMENTS

DON'T LOOK BACK

*But I focus on this one thing: Forgetting
the past and looking forward to what
lies ahead. I press on to reach the
end of the race and receive the heavenly
prize for which God, through
Christ Jesus is calling us.*

PHILIPPIANS 3:13B-14

One of Satan's favorite tools is a foreboding spirit, which is an anticipation of something negative. Instead of great expectations, someone with a foreboding spirit anticipates negative outcomes. They assume that even if things are good, something bad is on its way. I've actually had people tell me that thinking this way helps them manage their disappointment. I'm telling you that it will cripple your spirit, your mind, and your body.

It's interesting that one of the most beloved and encouraging verses in all of the Bible is found right after one of the most depressing verses in all of the Bible. This tells me that, yes, the struggle is real. But it also tells me that you can sort through the rubble and find glorious victory in Jesus. In Lamentations

3:19-20 the prophet says, "The thought of my suffering and homelessness is bitter beyond words. I will never forget this awful time, as I grieve over my loss." Eeyore, himself, could not have been more depressing.

When you only remember the bad times, hopelessness is always the result. It traps you in an emotional prison. But praise God, "He's a prison-shaking Savior!" And in Lamentations, it is as if Jeremiah was taken by the shoulders and shaken by the Holy Spirit. His tone takes a sudden and drastic turn for the better. He snaps out of his negative stupor and refuses to be defeated by the enemy of his soul and the memory of his past. He stirs himself and says, "Yet I still dare to hope." And my prayer for you is that no matter what happened yesterday, you can say today, "Yet I still dare to hope."

Jeremiah tells the reason for his hope. After the two most depressing verses, he pens two of the most inspiring verses in the entire Bible. They have, in fact, become the favorite verses of millions of saints. In a dramatic switch, he says, "The faithful love of the LORD never ends! His mercies never cease. Great is His faithfulness; His mercies begin afresh each morning" (Lamentations 3:22-23). Mike and I even had the timeless hymn based on these verses sung at our wedding, "Great Is Thy Faithfulness." What is so encouraging to me is that these verses aren't written by someone who had never been through hard times. These verses are penned by someone who chose not to be led by his emotions, but to instead base His hope on the truth of God's unfailing love.

You, too, should have a short memory about the sadness of yesterday and a long memory about God's faithfulness. His mercies are indeed new every morning. Rebuke your foreboding spirit. It is not from God. Get up each day and proclaim, "This is the day the LORD has made. We will rejoice and be glad in it" (Psalm 118:24). If you tried something yesterday that didn't work, try it again. However, this time, you will have more wisdom and experience. Don't determine how your day is going to go based on how you feel emotionally when you get up. Emotions follow truth, they never determine it. Just do what you know is right. Your emotions will catch up. And never let hurt feelings simmer in your soul. When you allow Christ to meet your needs, you can allow His love to cover a multitude of other people's sins. Give the gift of a fresh start to both you and everyone else who may have offended you.

Even if your last step was a misstep, always take the next step God has for you. Take it without reservation. Take it despite what happened yesterday. Take it despite your previous results. Take it despite that person who just hurt your feelings. "His mercies begin afresh each morning!"

Trust God when you don't feel like it. Trust God when you do feel like it. Trust God until you feel like it. Take the next step. Don't look back. That may be fearful for you, but wherever it may lead, God is already there waiting. He knows the way because He's gone before. If you trust your instincts concerning the future based on failures of the past, you could be in for a long and painful detour.

....

"Sorrow looks back; worry looks
around; but faith looks up"

ADRIAN ROGERS

YOU ARE IN
A BATTLE

The Spirit who lives in you is greater
than the spirit who lives in the world.

1 JOHN 4:4B

When you make the decision to follow Christ, you are literally signing up for a fight. You no longer operate in anonymity. You are out in the open as an enemy of the world and the world system.

I can't remember a time when this has been truer than it is today. Lines are drawn in the sand. You have become the mortal enemy of Satan himself. His goal is to take you down every chance he gets. He will bombard you with lies and deception. And if he can't get through to you, he will go after your children and your grandchildren.

I cannot warn you strongly enough that you should not begin a single day without first putting on the full armor of God. You should not even eat breakfast without being armored up. You should arm yourself and bind Satan and the forces of evil before you do anything else. You can do it in the shower. You can do it while you are getting dressed. You can do it while you are putting on your makeup.

The good news is that though you are signing up for a fight, you are signing up on the winning side. Jesus is stronger than Satan. It will be a battle. There will be setbacks. At times you will temporarily fail and fall. But you will get back up and you will win. Following Christ doesn't mean that troubles will go away. It means that Jesus will go through the troubles with you.

And that is exactly what will happen. You will go through your troubles. You won't go around them. You will go through them, but you will come out on the other side victorious. God will show you His power. He will show you His sufficiency. He will shower His grace down on you. You will come out with a testimony, a confidence, and an unshakeable faith. It's going to be a battle. But God Himself will fight the battle for you and you will win. First Chronicles 28:20a says, "Be strong and courageous and do the work! Don't be afraid or discouraged, for the LORD God, my God, is with you. He will not fail you or forsake you."

You are fighting a battle, but you are fighting a battle that's already been won. Satan doesn't want you to know that. He is bluffing you with cards he doesn't hold. Put on your armor and call his hand.

....

**"If the devil never bothers you
it's because you are both going in
the same direction. Turn around
and you'll meet him head on."**

ADRIAN ROGERS

THE MOST IMPORTANT PERSON IN YOUR DAY

Don't be selfish; don't try to impress others. Be humble, thinking of others as better than yourselves. Don't look out only for your own interest, but take an interest in others, too. You must have the same attitude that Christ Jesus had. Though He was God, He did not think of equality with God as something to cling to. Instead, He gave up His divine privileges; He took the humble position of a slave.

PHILIPPIANS 2:3-7A

If you want people to love you, don't make anything about loving you. The rarest gift you could possess is the gift of being able to make everyone else feel as if they are the most important person in the world. People will love you when you do. A simple rule to get along with anybody is to make it all about them, no matter who they are, and not all about you, no matter who you are. Frederick L. Collins is credited with saying, "There are two types of people who enter a room. One who says, 'Here I am,' and the other who says, 'There you are.'"

Throughout Scripture, the disciples were constantly trying to play bodyguard to Jesus. They didn't get what Jesus was about. They were constantly trying to keep people they perceived as being insignificant away from Him. Matthew 19:13-14 says: "One day some parents brought their children to Jesus so He could touch and bless them. But the disciples scolded the parents for bothering Him. When Jesus saw what was happening, He was angry with His disciples. He said to them, 'Let the children come to Me. Don't stop them! For the Kingdom of Heaven belongs to those who are like these children.' And He placed His hands on their heads and blessed them before He left."

Again, in Matthew 15:22-23: "A Gentile woman who lived there came to Him, pleading, 'Have mercy on me, O Lord, Son of David! For my daughter is possessed by a demon that torments her severely.'" Once again, the disciples urged Him to send her away. "'Tell her to go away,' they said. 'She is bothering us with all her begging.'"

Let me tell you that the people you deem to be insignificant do not get in the way of what God has called you to do. Rather, they are the reason He has called you. The task you are so busy doing is never the end goal. Who you stop and minister to while you are doing the task is what it is all about. In Luke 4:18 Jesus said: "The Spirit of the LORD is upon Me, for He has anointed Me to bring Good News to the poor. He has sent me to proclaim that captives will be released, that the blind will see, and the oppressed will be set free."

When you see others through the eyes of Jesus, you will find that the less important they are to others, the more important they are to God. Jesus loves the downtrodden, the helpless, and the poor. The way to show your love for Him is by loving the people that He loves.

....

"William Booth founded the Salvation Army. They were having a great convention and wanted the old general to come, but he was too sick and worn to attend. They said, 'Then send us a letter, a telegram, anything we can read to the convention.' He sent a one-word telegraph. It simply read: 'Others!'"

ADRIAN ROGERS

HALLELUJAH,
THE ANSWER IS NO

And the Holy Spirit helps us in our
weakness. For example, we don't know
what God wants us to pray for. But the
Holy Spirit prays for us with groaning
that cannot be expressed in words.
And the Father who knows all hearts
knows what the Spirit is saying, for
the Spirit pleads for us believers in
harmony with God's own will.

ROMANS 8:26-27

When you pray, are you just as happy with a no as you are with a yes? If you aren't, that tells me that your prayers are more you telling God what to do, rather than asking Him what He desires. A no could possibly be an answer from God saying that He has something even better. Being happy with that is a sign that you trust Him.

When you look back, many times it is obvious why God said no. It might have been a self-centered demand that was completely outside of His will. Or, you may have had your heart set on a piece of junk

57

that would have resulted in a waste of your time and resources. Other times, God may have said no to something He knew would eventually draw your heart away from Him. He knows you better than you know yourself. He also knows the future. Why would you not trust the One who loves you, knows what is best for you, and knows what is coming in your future?

The Children of Israel threw a temper tantrum in the wilderness when God said no. Psalm 106:14-15 says: "In the wilderness their desires ran wild, testing God's patience in that dry wasteland. So, He gave them what they asked for, but He sent a plague along with it." The King James Version says, "He gave them their request; but sent leanness into their soul." Mark 8:36 asks: "And what do you benefit if you gain the whole world but lose your own soul?"

There was an old television series in the 50s called "Father Knows Best." I'm sure there are many feminists today who wouldn't even want to see this charming show because of the title. But one thing is for sure, your earthly father may not always know best, but your Heavenly Father always does. Prayer isn't presenting God with your Christmas wishes or giving God a list of your requirements. Prayer is seeking His face and finding out what He wants. It is aligning your will with His, not trying to twist His will to give you your list of toys. Asking for God's will to be done on earth as it is in heaven, is getting your heart so in tune with His, that the desires of your heart are His desires. That's the prayer that will always get a yes. When you get to know God's heart you will know what He is all about making happen.

....

"The prayer that gets to heaven is the prayer that starts in heaven."

ADRIAN ROGERS

OUT OF THE NEST

But those who trust in the LORD will find new strength. They will soar high on wings like eagles. They will run and not grow weary. They will walk and not faint.

ISAIAH 40:31

The mother eagle skillfully and lovingly constructs a comfortable home for her new babies. She creates a strong foundation of sharp branches and twigs. It needs to withstand the elements. But although they make a fine foundation, they would not be an acceptable bed for her precious little ones. So, with her eagle eyes, she finds a puff of cotton here, and a touch of lint there. She meticulously covers every sharp, pointed object that might cause the slightest bit of discomfort. It's the life! I'm certain those little eaglets are thinking what a wonderful mother they have. How blessed they are that she would make them so comfortable and secure.

But then one day, something dreadfully different happens. In the same way that the mother eagle meticulously padded the nest with soft objects, she suddenly begins to methodically remove anything comfortable. Her previous kindness has seemingly turned to cruelty. There is nothing but pain left in the once comfortable home.

In fact, the sharp branches hurt so badly that the babies jump out of the nest to what they assume will be their death. They are in a desperate free-fall; but just before they crash the mother eagle swoops under them, catches them on her back, and takes them back up to the nest to repeat the process over again. It seems like the most perverted form of cruelty.

After many hurtful repeated episodes, they realize they can stretch their wings. They find that they can fly! And not just fly, they can soar! Their life wasn't over, after all. It was beginning. They only become the majestic bird they were meant to become, because the same mother who made them comfortable, made them uncomfortable. In her wisdom and love, she knew it was the only way. If she had allowed them to stay in the nest, they would have never learned to soar. And they certainly would have been eaten by a predator.

I think you see the analogy. God is like the mother eagle. On your own, you don't have the strength to leave your comfort zone and become all He intends you to become. Sometimes He has to do it for you, and sometimes He has to do it *to* you.

Even in your pain, can you submit to His discipline? He is teaching you to fly. Hosea 6:1 says: "Come, let us return to the LORD. He has torn us to pieces; now He will heal us. He has injured us; now He will bandage our wounds." He has hurt you in order to heal you. You have to trust.

....

"Even when you don't feel loved, God loves you."

ADRIAN ROGERS

WALKING WITH GOD

"Take My yoke upon you. Let Me teach
you, because I am humble and gentle at
heart, and you will find rest for your
souls. For My yoke is easy to bear
and my burden is light."

MATTHEW 11:29-30

Pounding pressure. Frazzled nerves. Frantic urgency. These are all symptoms that your life is out
of rhythm. They are flashing red lights on your
emotional dashboard. John Mason, in his book, "An
Enemy Called Average," said: "God is a planner, a
strategist. He is incredibly organized and has a
definite pace. More like a marathon runner than a
sprinter, He has our whole lives in mind, not just
tomorrow. Pressure usually accompanies us when
we are out of the pace of God."

Read that last line again, "Pressure usually accompanies us when we are out of the pace of God."
I've felt that pressure many times. It grabs me like
a fist right in the middle of my chest.

My husband, Mike, has much longer legs than
I do and a lot more energy. If we are not careful our
walks that are intended for intimate fellowship end
up with Mike so far in front that I would have to
shout to carry on that conversation. I have to grab
his hand to remind him to walk at my pace. I have
always loved the beautiful poem by Albert Camus,
"Don't walk behind me; I may not lead. Don't walk in
front of me; I may not follow. Just walk beside me and
be my friend." Well, most of the time I have loved the
poem. Sometimes, I like the version a cynic wrote:
"Don't walk behind me; I may not lead. Don't walk in
front of me; I may not follow. Don't walk beside me
either. Just leave me alone!" When I like that version
best, that's when I know I need to check the red lights
on my own emotional dashboard!

Rachel-Ruth Lotz Wright in the book, "Jesus
Followers—Igniting Faith in the Next Generation"
recounted the story of the Old Testament hero,
Enoch. It is one of the most amazing stories in the
Bible. Genesis 5:23-24 says, "Enoch lived 365 years,
walking in close fellowship with God. Then one day
he disappeared, because God took him." What?! That
sounds like the script out of a sci-fi movie. Did you
catch it? He never died! He just disappeared. It's as if
God said, "We've been walking together for so long
that you are a lot closer to My home than to yours."

In this day and age, it seems that ministers fall
one after another. The Christian world holds its
breath. Rachel-Ruth says something so simple and
yet so profound. She says that the secret of walking
with someone is simply walking at the same pace and

in the same direction. Enoch did that without wavering for 300 years. And we were impressed with how long Forrest Gump ran! What a personal challenge. I have a hard time keeping my focus for a week.

There are many times when God has to grab my hand and say, "Slow down, you are walking too fast. We are fellowshipping, not racing." You and I need to learn to relax in the presence of God. Take a deep breath. Exhale the concerns of your day by giving your burdens to Him. Exhale the sins in your heart by confessing and forsaking them. Inhale the sweet infilling of the Holy Spirit and the calmness of His presence. Learn to take leisurely strolls with Him in the cool of the evening where "He walks with you and He talks with you and He tells you, you are His own."

When you feel stressed, can you take that as an invitation to stop what you are doing? Can you put it all down and respond to His invitation to "Walk with Me. Talk with me?" You might even want to do that right now.

....

"When God develops inner character, He is never in a hurry."

ADRIAN ROGERS

YOU ARE
BEING LIED TO

He was a murderer from the beginning.
He has always hated the truth because
there is no truth in him. When he lies,
it is consistent with his character; for
he is a liar and the father of lies.

JOHN 8:44B

How would it affect you to find out that some of the things you have believed are not true? What if you found that you have an enemy who has been systematically brainwashing you? What would you do with that information? How would you combat it?

You do have an enemy named Satan who is intentionally lying to you. He only speaks one language, and everything he tells you is a lie. His target is your mind. He knows that when he controls your mind, he controls your beliefs. The frightening thing is that a false belief holds just as much power over your actions as a true belief. The only way to combat a false belief is with the truth. Darkness can only be defeated by light. But, hallelujah, it is always defeated by light!

How do you know if a thought comes from God, yourself, or demonic forces? If any thought is destructive, defeating, depressing, or divisive you can assume it is not from God. The Scriptures say that Satan's objective is "to kill, steal and destroy" (John 10:10). When your mind believes a lie, it causes you to act in ways that kill your relationships, steal your joy, and destroy your hope. His mission is accomplished.

Satan's goal is for the lies he speaks to take root and become a part of your mind's default pathways. When that happens, they become part of the very fabric of who you are.

This is warfare! You must take the offensive by proactively, immediately, and intentionally replacing those lies with truth each time they enter your mind. This must be done within seconds before they have a chance to take root. It can only be done through the truth of Scripture. It is not enough to recognize and challenge the lie. You must also replace the lie with the truth. The truth must be emphasized with the same power the lie was emphasized. It must be repeated often enough to form a new default pathway in your brain. This takes work. It is intentional. Lazy minds are the devil's delight.

When you memorize and meditate on the truth, your mind is transformed, and your thoughts become the thoughts of Christ. The ruts that your thoughts automatically go to in your mind become pathways of truth rather than pathways of lies. Your thoughts are transformed into correct beliefs, which result in correct actions. Your relationships are strengthened, your joy is returned, and your hope is restored.

Only you know where you are the most vulnerable. You must arm yourself with specific and targeted Scriptures that counteract the particular lies you believe. You can take screenshots of those verses on your phone. You can write them on notecards and put them on a ring clip. They are the antidotes to poison darts that are aimed at your unsuspecting mind all throughout your day. You must make the effort to find and take those screenshots. You must take the time to handwrite those Scriptures on notecards you can carry with you. You must "Stay alert! Watch out for your great enemy, the devil. He prowls around like a roaring lion, looking for someone to devour" (1 Peter 5:8). Never put your mind on autopilot. Always think about what you are thinking. There is never a time when your mind is not Satan's target. Whenever it is left unguarded, he seizes the opportunity and opens fire. The hardest work you should do every day is the work of guarding your mind by intentional thinking.

You hold the remote control to operate the channel guide in your mind. You can change that channel. But you must intentionally do so.

Jesus warned us when He said of Satan, "He was a murderer from the beginning. He has always hated the truth because there is no truth in him. When he lies, it is consistent with his character; for he is a liar and the father of lies" (John 8:44b).

....

"Satan is a clever liar because his lies sound so much like the truth. He wants to change your thought processes in order to deceive you and destroy you. He is not only the father of lies, but he lies about the biggest subject—God."

ADRIAN ROGERS

ARE YOU ASKING
GOD TO RIDE
ALONG WITH YOU?

*"So why do you keep calling Me 'Lord,
Lord!' when you don't do what I say?"*

LUKE 6:46

In the book, "All In," Mark Batterson said, "Most people may think they are following Jesus, but the reality is this: they have invited Jesus to follow them. They call Him Savior; they've never surrendered to Him as Lord. And I was one of them. Trust me, I didn't want to go anywhere without Jesus right there behind me. But I wanted Jesus to follow me, to serve my purposes, to do my will."

What Batterson said is very convicting. That is the story of much of the church in America today. They are unaware that they are doing anything wrong. But Jesus isn't someone you invite to ride with you while you run your errands. You don't set the agenda, He does. You don't make your goals and ask Him to bless them. You don't decide your plans and ask for His help to make them happen. That isn't how it works.

You and I are to come to God completely empty of our own desires. Our only desire should be to be so empty that when we allow Him to fill us, there is nothing inside of us except for Him. We don't dictate anything. All we do is report for duty. That's it. Period.

This is so opposite of what our flesh wants. We try to live our lives according to everything that makes us happy, and we try to control everything we want to happen. We sprinkle God on top of it all like He is salt and pepper. But God Almighty isn't a condiment, a good buddy, or a genie. He is King of kings and Lord of lords. The only way we are acceptable to Him is when we come in humility and total surrender. Surrender is the keyword. He doesn't exist to help us. We were created solely for His pleasure. We only exist to glorify Him and do His will.

It is possible that your day may look exactly the same to an outside observer. You may still run to the grocery and the gas station. Hopefully, you will still pick up the kids after school. I am talking about an inward attitude of complete surrender. You are still doing what you are doing. But you are doing it with a conscious dependence on His presence. He is inhabiting your body and speaking His thoughts into you, instead of hanging out alongside of you and listening to your opinions. Obviously, when God is your pilot and not your passenger, your schedule is interruptible at any time. Make your day all about pleasing Him, instead of hoping that He will rubberstamp your plans.

....

"If He is not your Lord, He is not your Savior."

ADRIAN ROGERS

I DIDN'T WANT TO
GO TO CHURCH

*I was glad when they said to me, "Let
us go to the house of the LORD."*

PSALM 122:1

This is going to be hard for some of you to believe since my father, Adrian Rogers, was also my pastor for most of my life. But for the majority of my life, I looked at church as more of a duty than a delight. It was a drudgery like going to school. And about the only thing worse than going to church was going to Sunday School. I'm not even sure where the Women's Ministry would rank, because I never went to find out. If it weren't for being forced by my parents to go, and then years later, trying to please my husband, I'm not certain I would've gone at all. If I had the option, like so many do today, I'm certain I would have chosen to just sit at home and watch "virtual church" on the television or the computer.

So, I'm not judging here. That was most of my life. And during the height of COVID, when the government duped us into shutting down our churches by calling it an unnecessary public gathering, I hate to admit that I was thrilled. I watched at home in my pajamas. It was kind of like background noise on my computer, while I was multitasking or playing computer games. That is very sobering for me to type, but it is true. In other words, my sole purpose was to check it off my spiritual to-do list.

But somehow, some way, God in His mercy has done a new work in my life. He had to do something drastic to get my attention. It's a long story, but He shut down what I was living for and left me with nothing but Himself. I had been a believer for years, yet I found myself coasting. God broke through. He came and found me when I wasn't looking for Him.

Now, there is no place I would rather be than in the house of the Lord. I love my church. I love my pastor. I love my life group class, a.k.a. Sunday School. I love my Women's Bible study class. I love the music. I love worshiping together with the people of God. I promise you that it is like I am listening to everything with brand-new ears and watching with brand-new eyes. I can hardly sit through a message without tears dripping down my cheeks. I can hardly sing a song without raising my hands in praise.

During the Covid lockdowns I convinced myself that there was no difference between sitting at home watching and being there in person watching. I'm sure it's because, either way, all I was doing was just watching. I was nothing more than a spectator. But when my desperate need forced me to find answers in the One who created me, I fell deeply in love with Jesus. And when I fell deeply in love with Jesus, I also fell deeply in love with His people and the place they gathered.

If you go to television church, or internet church, or no church at all, I'm here to tell you that there is power in the body of Christ. "For where two or three gather together as my followers, I am there among them" (Matthew 18:20). We are told in Scripture, "And let us not neglect our meeting together, as some people do, but encourage one another, especially now that the day of His return is drawing near" (Hebrews 10:25).

If you don't go to church or don't want to go, and there isn't a physical reason that makes it impossible, I'm going to tell you from experience that there is a stronghold somewhere in your life. I had a bunch of them. I finally learned how to gain victory. And with every chain that broke, it was replaced by an overwhelming desire to spend private devotional time with Jesus, coupled with an equally overwhelming desire to spend public time united with the people of God in corporate worship.

....

"If your faith can't get you to church on Sunday, I doubt it will get you into heaven."

ADRIAN ROGERS

HOW TO HAVE
PERFECT PEACE

"You will keep in perfect peace
all who trust in You, all whose
thoughts are fixed on You!"

ISAIAH 26:3

Worry is the opposite of perfect peace. Fear is the opposite of perfect peace. Resentment is the opposite of perfect peace. Unforgiveness is the opposite of perfect peace. When peace isn't there, it can feel like the churning of a tumultuous sea. The tightness in your chest can make you wonder if you are having a heart attack. You can feel the queasiness in your stomach and the dull ache in the back of your head. And all that is nothing compared to the restlessness in your spirit. When nothing seems to be going right, how do you come to a place of perfect peace? How do you experience that peace when the shape of what you want to be happening in your life doesn't fit into the shape of what seems to be happening in your life?

If you are anything like me, there are times when unwanted situations come at you against your will. When that happens you need to respond, rather than react. In the midst of the stress, it seems that it is almost impossible to choose your response. But that is exactly what you have to do. You have to choose. You have to choose to trust God. Trust God despite your feelings and despite your circumstances. You must literally choose to fix your thoughts on Him (Philippians 4:8). When I think of the word "fix" I like to think of it as setting your thoughts in concrete.

This is never a passive reaction. It is a resolute choice. It is a choice that is decided on long before you are in the middle of an "event." If you wait until something is happening to you, your emotions will win every time. You have to build a tornado shelter long before the actual tornado is upon you. Your mind has to be resolutely set in concrete before the stressful episode ever takes place. You have to decide in advance how you are going to respond.

That really shouldn't be as hard as it is. Unfortunately, we have many wrong perceptions and prejudices that are fixed in our minds. It seems that no amount of reasoning will change them. Why are we able to do this negatively, but not positively? I've often thought that worry and meditation on God's word are two sides of the same coin. They are both bringing up a thought over and over again throughout the day. One causes your problem, while the other solves it. It certainly is easier to do the worrying than the meditation.

As I have written before, most people just think whatever thought the devil gives them to think. They don't change it. They don't challenge it.

One of the most revolutionary truths you can learn is that you can choose thoughts and you can reject thoughts. Satan doesn't want you to realize that you hold a remote control in your hand. You must learn this! Don't fix your thoughts on your bank account. Don't fix your thoughts on your circumstances. Don't fix your thoughts on someone who disappoints you. Trust God, fix your thoughts on Jesus, and release the results to Him.

This is what I do when I am stressed. I take a few deep breaths. Then I pray something like, "Jesus, You are Lord over this situation. You are all-powerful. I know You love me with everlasting love. I can trust You. I do trust You. I ask You to take care of me and lead me into green pastures and beside still waters."

When I feel my emotions churning within me, that is a signal that there is something I have not given over to the Holy Spirit. When the Spirit has full control, there is always peace. This peace is symbolized in Psalm 23 as being led beside still waters. So, the question I ask is, "Am I experiencing churning waters, or still waters? Am I in charge of my life, or is the Shepherd leading me?

When the Shepherd leads, the peace will flow. As a matter of fact, it will be perfect (John 14:27).

....

"Christ won't transform my problem until I transfer it to Him."

ADRIAN ROGERS

HE SEES, HE CARES

*I will be glad and rejoice in Your unfailing
love, for You have seen my troubles, and
You care about the anguish of my soul.*

PSALM 31:7

As a good friend, there are two things I want from
you when I have needs and hurts. I want you to see
what is happening to me. I want you to be sensitive
and aware when I am hurting. Maybe it shouldn't, but
it would wound my spirit if you were so self-absorbed
that you didn't even notice. Even if it is only for a
brief moment, I want you to look up from your world
and enter into mine. And I not only want you to see,
I want you to care. You may not have any answers.
You probably won't. I don't expect you to. But even if
you have no idea what to say, I will still be secure in
your love if I know that you see and feel that you care.

When you think about it, that's probably the same
thing you want from your friend. There are many
times they do come through for you, or you probably
wouldn't consider them a friend. But they are human. And at some time, all friends will disappoint.
Unfortunately, there is a good possibility that the

friend you are counting on will be preoccupied and insensitive when you need them the most. There's a good chance they will have too many problems of their own to get involved in yours. There is no lonelier feeling than feeling unseen by your own friend. I want to tell you that you will save yourself a lot of hurt if you will learn that God didn't create any friend to be everything to you. It doesn't matter who they are. That position is reserved for God alone.

If you put your hope in any earthly relationship, at some point, you are going to be hurt. The deep needs of your heart can only be fully met in Christ. He is the only One who will never let you down. And oh, "What a friend we have in Jesus!"

David said in Psalm 31:7: "I will be glad and rejoice in Your unfailing love, for You have seen my troubles, and You care about the anguish of my soul."

The Scriptures are full of paradoxes. And there is a paradox when it comes to relationships. When your relationships take second place, they actually become better than when they take first place. When you put your relationship with Christ before your relationships with your friends, you will actually become a better friend. You will become that friend who does both see and care. Christ will fill you so full that you will overflow love and compassion into the lives of those around you. You won't be so desperate to get your own needs met that you can't focus on the needs of others. It's like eating from a buffet. I'm always free to share my food if I know I can go back for more.

The song is true, you HAVE been looking for love in all the wrong places. Put your hope in Jesus. He sees, He knows, He cares! There is never a time when you are alone. There is never a time when there is no one who cares. There is never a situation where you are hopeless. Look in the right place. When you do, you will realize that you already have a true Friend. And in addition, your true Friend, Jesus, will fill you with what you need to be able to be a friend to others. That's a win-win!

....

"God is searching our hearts in order to supply our deepest need."

ADRIAN ROGERS

THE FUTILITY OF
TRYING HARDER

"Those who remain in Me, and I in
them, will produce much fruit.
For apart from Me you can do nothing."

JOHN 15:5B

It isn't your imagination. You can't do anything! You read that right. If you suck it up and dig deeper all you will find is more dirt. You don't have the ability. You don't have the right words. You don't possess the power to force anything good to happen. It is futile. The harder you try, the more you will bang your head against a wall. You will always come up short.

I know you are checking the cover of this book right now to see if it was authored by Debbie Downer. But could it be that this depressing news is actually cause for rejoicing? In your failure, you can find freedom! Hopefully, when you experience futility after futility, it will finally result in the revelation that victory comes by emptying yourself, instead of reloading and trying harder. When you realize that, what a gloriously freeing day it will be! You don't become strong until you come to the end of your strength!

Don't be discouraged. Just wait! The script is about to be flipped! When your desperate failure and futility cause you to finally seek the power of Christ to fill your emptiness, then your body will become nothing more than clothes for God to wear. He will inhabit you and perform miracles on your behalf. You will become victorious the moment He begins to do His work through you, instead of you trying in vain to do it for Him. That, my friend, is a transformational thought!

He has been waiting for you to give up. What joy there is in hearing Him say that you can stop trying to do more. What freedom there is in finding out that you don't need to work harder. All He wants is for you to wave the white flag of surrender. He asks that you give Him the one thing you so fight to keep for yourself--control. This control issue you have is a big deal. When you retain control, it means that you are the lord of your own life. And *the* Lord will always fight against a competing lord. But, when He is in control, when He is the supreme Lord of your life, something incredible happens. He stops fighting against you, and He begins to fight for you.

God says: "'My grace is all you need. My power works best in weakness.' So now I am glad to boast about my weaknesses, so that the power of Christ can work through me. For when I am weak, then I am strong" (2 Corinthians 12:9, 10b).

What an incredible truth! There is freedom that results from your failure. God causes all things to work together for your good (Romans 8:28). God's power works best in your weakness (2 Corinthians 12:9). Your self-effort only dilutes His strength. When it becomes "none of you" and "all of Him," you will begin to experience victory after victory. Strongholds will collapse. Giants will fall. You've been going at it all wrong. When you give up, you will go up. Victory comes through surrender.

....

"What we surrender, God takes.
What He takes, He cleanses.
What He cleanses, He fills.
What He fills, He uses."

ADRIAN ROGERS

A BETTER WAY TO LEAD

Patience can persuade a prince, and
soft speech can break bones.

PROVERBS 25:15

I am drawn to the subject of leadership. I like to study it and talk about it. Over the years, I've led many people with success. However, the hardest person I've ever had to lead was myself. I'm going to make myself very vulnerable and unzip my outer shell in order to allow you to look deep inside. Because I think it may help you, I'm going to take a risk and let you see some character flaws that I kept hidden from those who only knew me from a distance. There are some things I have been very good at doing, but I was woefully lacking in the most important set of leadership qualities. Truthfully, I built what seemed like a well-respected business. But in the second half of my life, looking back, I have realized that many of the most important qualities of servant-leadership were too often lacking.

As you painfully look inside of me, you may recognize some of these same areas of need inside of you. The qualities that I missed in the first half of my life aren't always talked about as being leadership qualities. But even though these qualities aren't generally associated with leadership, if you don't have them, no one will follow you for long. The cracks will eventually begin to show and people will begin to leave. And, if you don't have lasting followers, you aren't a legacy leader. That's plain and simple.

The qualities are kindness, gentleness, humility, and graciousness. Unfortunately, these qualities are often lacking in the segment of society that is most often associated with leadership, the "Cholerics." I know what I'm talking about. "I are one!" If you look up "choleric" in a dictionary, you will find my picture! And if you are a choleric like me, and you don't allow the Holy Spirit to add kindness, gentleness, humility, and graciousness into the mix, you aren't going to lead people; you are only going to alienate them.

Let's get started with some hard truths. I'm going to use the word "you" in most of these truths, but remember that the person who needs this most is me!

Telling people what to do is not effective. It is offensive. No one wants to be told what to do. They want servant leadership, not dictatorship.

Using strong language to make a point only turns people off and offends their sensibilities. People seek shelter from a blast. They are never drawn to it.

When someone doesn't understand what you are saying, accusing them of being stupid doesn't do anything to motivate them to learn. It only motivates them to stay away from you. I hope you and I can both realize that if someone has a different opinion than ours, that doesn't make them stupid. If you act like they are, you will have completely lost your ability to win them over.

If someone doesn't do what you think they should do, it doesn't make them lazy. Far too many times, it just means you didn't do a good job of motivating them.

Sarcasm is not an effective motivational tool. The only point it makes is that you are a toxic person who will hurt others.

Abruptness does not promote connection or conversation. It makes people feel devalued. It makes people feel like their thoughts and feelings are not important. It makes people feel used. You got what *you* needed and now you are done.

People will forgive almost anything except for arrogance. No one has a problem with people who make mistakes. Everyone has a problem with people who feel like they don't.

If you want to make people pay, teach them a lesson, put them in their place, or make them feel like they made you feel, you will become a miserable person. Not only will you be eaten up with bitterness, but no one will want to entrust themselves to you. They are not willing to pay the payment you will extract if they make a mistake.

Smugness does not prove a point. It only makes people want to slap you. If you are prone to that "smug" look, you will stand a better chance of people following you if you are wearing a paper sack over your face. Your face can turn people off without saying a word. You cannot lead or influence a person who is turned off by you. If you don't know what "that look" is, I'm sure your spouse does. Ask them.

Everyone operates better in an atmosphere of praise than they do in an atmosphere of guilt. One of the best mantras to live life by was written by Ken Blanchard in his classic book, "The One Minute Manager." He said "Catch someone in the act of doing something right and tell them about it."

Being opinionated is the opposite of being teachable. Even if you are correct, if you say it in such a way that puts everyone else down, no one will take your side.

People are more drawn to the way you care about them, than by what you say to them or what you have achieved. They will only follow someone who makes it all about them, instead of all about you.

Power is found in gentleness. Jesus said, "The meek will inherit the earth" (Matthew 5:5). People will still follow you through mistakes you make if you are humble. Graciousness creates an atmosphere to which people will flock.

If people are resisting your leadership, it is time to look inside. And the "you" that I've been referring to is directed toward me, Gayle Foster. I hope you have been helped by reading the private notes I wrote for my own benefit. Do you see anywhere you can improve along with me? Wouldn't it be incredible if the people you are leading actually liked you? Wouldn't it be even more incredible if you could use your influence to make them want to know more about Jesus?

....

"Failure is not final."

ADRIAN ROGERS

IN THE MIDST
OF THE CHAOS

*Jesus took Peter, John, and James up on
a mountain to pray. Suddenly, two men,
Moses and Elijah, appeared and began
talking with Jesus. They were glorious
to see. Peter, not even knowing what
he was saying, blurted out, "Master,
it is wonderful for us to be here! Let's
make three shelters as memorials." The
next day, after they had come down the
mountain, a large crowd met Jesus. A
man in the crowd called out to Him,
"Teacher, I beg You to look at my son,
my only child. An evil spirit keeps
seizing him, making him scream."*

LUKE 9:28B, 30-31A, 33B, 37-39A

I just read something extremely convicting out of
"My Utmost for His Highest." I'm going to get to what
Oswald Chambers said, but first, let me tell you a little
bit about the situation I was in when I wrote this.
At the time I was writing, my son, his wife, and my
three very young grandchildren (five, three, and one)

were living in my house. They were there for about six months while extensive repair work was being done at their home. The desire of my heart is to have intimate fellowship with God. But at that time every square inch of my house was loud and chaotic. There was NOTHING monastic about my home! Nothing!

In the midst of the chaos, I came to understand this stark reality: Anyone can be "spiritual" in the absence of noise, conflict, and clutter. Is that really spirituality, or is it only like a new car on a showroom floor that hasn't yet been taken for a test drive?

True Christianity is never intended to be lived in isolation. Jesus lived His life surrounded by contagious lepers and screaming demoniacs. He filled Himself daily with the power and presence of His Father in order to be able to walk through this sin-filled world and give Himself to people who were broken, hurting, and needy. He never isolated Himself from the people He came to seek and to save, except for times to recharge and refuel.

This is what Oswald Chambers said: "The secret of a Christian's life is that the supernatural becomes natural in him as a result of the grace of God, and the experience of this becomes evident in the practical, everyday detail of life, not in times of intimate fellowship with God. And when we come in contact with things that create confusion and a flurry of activity, we find to our own amazement that we have the power to stay wonderfully poised even in the center of it all."

Does that hit you the way it hits me? Poised in the midst of confusion and a flurry of activity! Wow!

My "religion" is of no use if it cannot be lived out in the chaotic noise and disorder of the very people Jesus came to seek and to save. I need to be divinely interruptible and supernaturally calm in the midst of the mess. Could it be that the people you may be trying to avoid are the only reason He has chosen to still leave you on this earth? (I'm not talking about my precious family, here. I'm not trying to avoid them). God has no human vessels that He fills for decorative purposes only. The only reason He fills me anew every day is to completely pour me out by the end of it.

Read Oswald Chambers' sentence again: "When we come in contact with things that create confusion and a flurry of activity, we find to our own amazement that we have the power to stay wonderfully poised even in the center of it all."

May I stay so filled with Jesus that I amaze even myself at how calm I have become, not only around my family and precious and loud grandchildren that I adore, but also around the people who have always irritated the fool out of me!

....

> ## "If you can be a Christian at home, you can be a Christian anywhere."
> ADRIAN ROGERS

24-HOUR CHALLENGE

The heart of the godly thinks
carefully before speaking.

PROVERBS 15:28A

I have been convicted about the negativity that continually comes out of my mouth. When I stop and carefully listen, it seems that way too many of the things I tend to verbalize are not positive. If I repeat something I've heard on the news, it will be something horrific. I am constantly alert to "catch" a politician doing something wrong. If I comment on the state of the economy, it is regarding inflation or a bear market. If I announce the upcoming weather, it is because there is rain in the forecast or a storm on the horizon. It seems that sometimes I am no more than a "gloom and doom announcer."

Far too many times, I am prone to tell what I don't like about someone rather than what I do like about them. I could go on and on, but I am depressing myself just thinking about it. I want to change. I want to speak life. I want to challenge you to see if you can go for an entire 24-hour period without verbalizing negativity. See if the atmosphere in your home doesn't change. If it does, then do it again the next day. And the next. Ephesians 4:29b says, "Let everything you say be good and helpful, so that your words will be an encouragement to those who hear them."

When the angels announced the birth of Christ to the shepherds they said, "Don't be afraid. I bring you good news that will bring great joy to all people" (Luke 2:10b). The very word "gospel" means "good news." Wouldn't your home be transformed if every time you opened your mouth you could say, "Don't be afraid that I am going to be critical. Actually, what I'm going to say is good news that will bring you great joy." You might have to revive a few people from shock.

Proverbs 15:28a says, "The heart of the godly thinks carefully before speaking." Negativity always repels. Positivity always attracts. Ephesians 5:18b-20 admonishes us to "Be filled with the Holy Spirit, singing psalms and hymns and spiritual songs among yourselves, and making music to the Lord in your hearts. And give thanks for everything to God the Father in the name of our Lord Jesus Christ." Do that, and your house will become a house of praise. Your family will love to see you coming!

....

"Don't go around looking like an advance agent for the undertaker."

ADRIAN ROGERS

IT'S THE
LITTLE THINGS

*And if you give even a cup of cold water
to one of the least of My followers,
you will surely be rewarded.*

MATTHEW 10:42

What if God isn't expecting you to do anything amazing, profound, or extraordinary today? That's His responsibility. What if all He needs you to be is faithful, kind, and gentle? What if you are waiting for a big assignment, or an impressive calling, when the actual calling from God is to minister to the sales lady helping you in the clothing department or the three-year-old trying to climb up in your lap?

You may be all dressed up in your fancy business attire, and you might have just closed two of the most profitable deals ever. Good for you if you did! I have yoga pants on, no makeup, and I just changed two of the foulest, stinkiest, most disgusting diapers ever. If we are doing what we are doing in His strength and for His glory, we are both doing exactly what God has called us to do today. One is not better than the other.

We make it far too hard. We think we need to come to Him as a theologian with a doctorate when He wants us to come as a little child. All you need to do is just do the next thing He has told you to do. It may be around the kitchen table or at the corporate office. Just have a tender and receptive spirit when He speaks. Just be kind and do good to the next person you see in the ordinary course of your day. Life is made of those ordinary days, not grand events. Anyone can rise to the occasion when the spotlight is on them. God is impressed with the things you do when there is no one looking and no one applauding.

I spend so much of my time thinking that God wants me to line up a speaking engagement or finish writing a book. All God is wanting me to do is be patient and gentle with my husband. Many times, the second thing is far more difficult to do than the first. There is no difference in what we perceive to be the sacred and the secular. There is no distinction between serving God in the simple and in the spectacular.

The truth of the matter is that too many times the grand things we think we are doing for God are the things that amount to nothing in the world to come. Let this sink in: "If I could speak all the languages of earth, and of angels, but didn't love others, I would only be a noisy gong or a clanging cymbal. If I had the gift of prophecy, and I understood all of God's secret plans and possessed all knowledge, and if I had such faith that I could move mountains, but didn't love others, I would be nothing. If I gave everything I have to the poor and even sacrificed my body, I could boast about it, but if I didn't love others, I would have gained nothing" (1 Corinthians 13:1-3).

On the other hand, Jesus said, "And if you give even a cup of cold water to one of the least of My followers, we will surely be rewarded" (Matthew 10:42). I can't even imagine what you will get for changing a disgusting diaper!

....

"In all spiritual things, we should be natural. And in all natural things we should be spiritual."

ADRIAN ROGERS

THE SECRET TO VICTORY

Are you defeated by the same sin in your life over and over again? In your mind, do you know that it is not "if" you are going to do the same thing again, it is only "how soon" you are going to do it again? Let's face it, it is bigger than you are. How do I know this? Trust me, I know.

If you are like me, that same attitude seems to come through every day. The scenarios may change, and the people may be different, but the attitude is constant. It will not change until you realize that it isn't your circumstances that cause the attitude. The attitude is on the inside. What happens to you only causes what's already inside of you to come out. In other words, what's down in the well comes up in the bucket.

Another place we are prone to be defeated is that it is easier to default to fear instead of trust. It doesn't matter how God provided last year or even last night. The very next time your security is threatened, you simply don't trust that God will take care of you. You panic and begin frantically preparing a backup plan, just in case He doesn't come through.

Let me tell you what happens when you do that. First of all, it is an insult to the Almighty God who "merely spoke and the heavens were created" (Psalm 33:6a). And secondly, you are giving the testimony to the onlooking world, that you really don't believe He cares or is capable. And yet, you do it every time. You do it regardless of what He has just done to meet your needs. Fear is the polar opposite response of someone who knows the character of God and trusts Him to keep His promises.

How do you gain victory over these problems that seem to be on a loop in your life?

If you are anything like me, I am certain that many times you want to throw up your hands in defeat. So many times I think that's just the way I am, and I need to resign myself to that fact. On the other hand, when. I'm not giving up, I'm doubling down. I am thinking that I need to make a conscious effort to try harder. I need more self-discipline. I need more willpower. Let me tell you, that hasn't worked either. It hasn't worked in the past and it isn't going to work in the future. In other words, it seems I will continue to fail and I will continue to beat myself up over it. In the past I thought I would go to my grave without ever experiencing the victory I heard other people talk about.

But praise God, I am finally learning a life-changing spiritual truth! In the latter part of my life, I have realized that victory over sinful actions and sinful attitudes has absolutely nothing to do with my willpower, or yours. Nothing! Christ has already won the victory I wasn't even capable of winning. If I had not learned to live in the reality of that victory, I would still be literally as hopeless as I felt.

If you, like me, will humbly come in emptiness to the cross, and by faith, claim what He has already done on your behalf, then a new power will come into play. You will be able to live in victory through what Christ has done for you, rather than through what you are trying so hard to do for yourself.

Philippians 4:13 says, "For I can do everything through Christ, who gives me strength." That means you can do nothing in your own strength, but you can do anything through HIS strength. And then Ephesians 1:19-20 tells what I think is one of the most awe-inspiring truths in the entire Bible. It says that the exact same power that raised Jesus from the dead now lives in you. That is, the power of the Holy Spirit of God Himself literally lives inside your body. Read that sentence again! No wonder you can do anything through Him who gives you strength.

You are wasting your time trying harder to gain victory. That is like running around your house lighting candles when you need to be turning on the light switch. The secret isn't in fighting harder; it is in surrendering. It is in letting go of your self-effort and staying in constant connectedness to the power available to you, Christ Himself. The Scripture calls that "abiding." That is not just your hope of victory; it is certain victory! Every time you allow Him to live His life through your surrendered body and sanctified will, you are going to win.

If it isn't working, it is because you haven't flipped the switch from your effort to His power. But when He is invited, He will always flow into and through an empty and surrendered vessel. You can begin right now to live a different life. The hopeless cycle can be broken. You can become a different person.

....

"Victory is not achieved by fighting. It is achieved by faith."

ADRIAN ROGERS

READ THIS
VERY SLOWLY

*Do not love this world nor the things
it offers you, for when you love the
world, you do not have the love of the
Father in you.*

1 JOHN 2:15

One very frightening time, in the middle of the night, I was awakened with my husband kneeling by the side of my bed. He held a cell phone in his hands and whispered to me, "Put your fingers on 9-1-1. Someone is definitely in our house and I'm going to find them." That will get your heart started! As it turns out, something was in our house, not someone. We had flying squirrels in our attic. But that's another story for another time. We probably had bats in the belfry as well!

Fast forward many years and my husband, Mike, came to me with the same urgency and told me to read 1 John 2:15-17 out loud and very slowly out of the New Living Translation. That doesn't happen but once every couple of decades, and so I did it. Now, I'm going to tell you to do the same thing. Read it out loud and very slowly. I've typed it out for you so that you don't even have to look it up. It is powerful in the King James Version, but it leaves no doubt in the New Living Translation!

"Do not love this world nor the things it offers you, for when you love the world, you do not have the love of the Father in you. For the world offers only a craving for physical pleasure, a craving for everything we see, and pride in our achievements and possessions. These are not from the Father but are from this world. And this world is fading away, along with everything that people crave. But anyone who does what pleases God will live forever" (1 John 2:15-17).

This hit me between the eyes. It is all there in black print on white paper, but how easy it is to miss. All the world offers is a craving for physical pleasure. That pleasure is only for a second, and afterward, your mouth is filled with gravel. It leaves you disappointed, disillusioned, and weighed down with guilt. Even the food you crave leaves you sick, unhealthy, and fat.

I have lived my life craving what I can see when the only things that bring lasting pleasure are the things I cannot see. I have lived my life trying to accumulate achievements and possessions without realizing that they are only things of this world. And this world is passing away.

"Turn your eyes upon Jesus. Look full in His wonderful face. And the things of earth will grow strangely dim in the light of His glory and grace."

The world does not understand this. It only understands physical pleasure. It only understands what can be seen with the eyes. We are not of this world. Our citizenship is in heaven. We serve a different King. We speak a different language. We have a different agenda. We have made the right choice.

....

"Anything you love more, fear more, serve more, or value more than God is your idol."

ADRIAN ROGERS

THE SECRET OF SILENCE

Let all that I am wait quietly before
God, for my hope is in Him.

PSALM 62:5

In "My Utmost for His Highest" Oswald Chambers talks about the intimacy of God's silence. Chambers said: "When you cannot hear God, you will find that He has trusted you in the most intimate way possible—with absolute silence, not a silence of despair, but one of pleasure because He saw that you could withstand an even bigger revelation."

For most of my life, I would have read that paragraph, and just have shaken my head saying, "I don't have a clue what on earth he is even talking about." But somehow, God has opened my once-hardened heart, and I actually understand what that paragraph means.

Right now I am in a place of holding. God isn't currently giving me a lot of clear answers. For the vast majority of my life that would have frustrated me beyond belief. I would have found myself whining, complaining, and arguing with the Almighty

Himself. I would have made myself busy, proactively lighting my own fires and strategizing my own backup plans. I would have marched ahead of God and run through roadblocks. I just know I would have. And I would have told you that if you weren't doing the same things yourself, you were complacent.

I know I am experiencing a major spiritual breakthrough, not because I am receiving answer after answer, but simply because I am content in the silence. It hasn't happened all at once. I went from trying to make things happen on my own, to trusting that God was preparing me for something that was coming. I told Him that I would faithfully prepare and be ready when that time came and His will was revealed. But the final step came when I realized that God's will wasn't something in the future. It is right here. Right now. Developing intimacy with Him is not merely something that prepares me for the next assignment. It is the assignment. It is the end goal. His purpose is for me to love Him, enjoy Him, and depend on Him right now.

I have a friend who lives out of town. She thinks that she needs to entertain me when I visit. She thinks she needs to find things for me to do that will make my trip worthwhile. I try to tell her that all I want to do is just to spend time with her. If we happen to go somewhere, it doesn't really matter to me where it is or what we do. I came to town just to be with her. That's all I care about. We may happen to get something else accomplished while I am there, but those are secondary and tertiary things.

From God's perspective waiting and silence are the ultimate acts of intimacy. Waiting means there is no rush to get on to the next thing. Silence means I am content in His presence. I am enjoying Him, not the movie we are going to see together or the store where we are going to shop. Those things will happen, but they aren't the ultimate. Sitting in contented silence is the ultimate. I know that He will care for me and I am content not knowing anything more. The most beautiful melody ever written is the sound of silence.

Psalm 46:10a, NASB says, "Cease striving and know that I am God." There could not be a way to say it better than the Psalmist. If you don't trust God to be God, you will always be striving. You will always be trying to figure it out and make something happen. Having to know, and wanting to be in control mean that you think you could do a better job being God. I have finally found that there is unspeakable peace in not having to know the answers because I know and trust God. There is actual joy in the silence. It is as if God is saying, "Relax. Don't even worry about it. I've got it covered." Matthew 11:28-30 says, "Then Jesus said, 'Come to Me, all of you who are weary and carry heavy burdens, and I will give you rest. Take My yoke upon you. Let Me teach you, because I am humble and gentle at heart, and you will find rest for your souls. For My yoke is easy to bear, and the burden I give you is light.'"

It hasn't been an easy road for an obsessive controller like me to get to this point. But I am making great progress. I am finally just like a little child who doesn't have to know anything, except that she is loved by her Father, who will take care of her. The most intimate place you can come to in your relationship with God is not when He tells you everything. It is when He doesn't have to. Just "Cease striving and know that He is God."

. . . .

**"I may know Him better,
but there's nothing better
than knowing Him."**

ADRIAN ROGERS

Precious friend,

The wisdom contained within this book will not make sense to you until you have repented of your sins and placed your faith in Christ for salvation.

When that takes place you will receive the forgiveness of your sins, a brand new beginning, and the power and the desire to live a holy life. Prayerfully and carefully read the words below that will tell you how to receive Christ and become what the Bible calls being born again. This can be the day your new life begins.

....

EVERYONE DIES

On that day, What will be your greatest need as you stand before God?

Did you know the Bible says you WILL stand before God and give an account for your life? (Heb. 9:27). In that day, God will judge the secrets of men by Jesus Christ..."(Romans 2:16).

Yes, **every secret sin** will be known. Everything! PLEASE Listen to your conscience. Have you ever lied? Stolen anything? Used God's name as a curse word? Hated someone? Looked with lust? Sex outside of marriage? Did you answer any of these questions YES? Please don't ignore your conscience or dismiss whatever comes to mind. The Bible says that God's law is written on each of our hearts, and **our conscience bears witness either accusing or else excusing** us.

(Romans 2:15) If you are guilty of breaking God's law (we ALL are), then God can justly punish you in Hell. He made the laws, and He is the Judge.

Question: Do you want God's justice and face your punishment, OR, Do you want His mercy, and be granted forgiveness?

This is where the "gospel" (Good News) begins to make sense. The Bible says that Jesus Christ came to earth TO SAVE SINNERS. He lived a perfect and sinless life...And that "God demonstrates His own love towards us in that while we were still sinners, Christ died for us." (Romans 5:8) Because of our sin against a Holy God, we owed a debt we couldn't pay....so Christ paid our debt in full on our behalf. "The wages of sin is death, but the gift of God is eternal life in Jesus Christ our Lord." (Romans 6:23).

Your greatest need is a Substitute for your punishment, and forgiveness from your sins. The Bible says that if you will confess that you have broken God's law by sinning against Him, Repent from your sins (turn from sin to God) and put your trust/faith in Jesus and what He did for you on the cross.... by dying in your place, taking on God's wrath, then rising from the grave and defeating the penalty of death, then God will forgive you and grant you eternal life as a free gift. (Mark 1:15) "For it is by grace you have been saved through faith, and that not of yourselves, it is the gift of God, not of works, lest anyone should boast." (Ephesians 2:8-9).

Repent, and place your faith in Jesus today!